curious about

TURTLES

T000504 7

BY ALISSA THIELGES

AMICUS

What are you

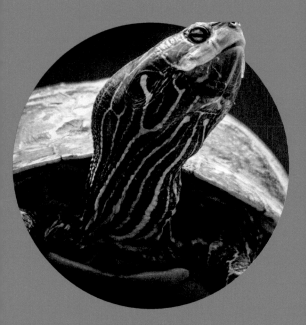

curious about?

CHAPTER THREE

3

Turtle Behavior

PAGE

16

Curious About is published by Amicus
P.O. Box 227
Mankato, MN 56002
www.amicuspublishing.us

Editor: Rebecca Glaser
Series Designer: Kathleen Petelinsek
Book Designer: Aubrey Harper
Photo Researchers: Alissa Thielges and Omay Ayres

Library of Congress Cataloging-in-Publication Data

Names: Thielges, Alissa, 1995- author.
Title: Curious about turtles / by Alissa Thielges.
Description: Mankato, Minnesota: Amicus,
[2023] | Series: Curious about
pets | Audience: Ages 6-9 | Audience: Grades 2-3 | Summary:
"Nine kid-friendly Q&As teach readers about life with a turtle,
including their behavior, aquarium needs, and how their shells
grow. Engaging questions draw in kids while research-based
answers satisfy their curiosity. Simple infographics support
visual learning. A Stay Curious! feature encourages kids to keep
asking questions and models media literacy skills. Includes table
of contents, glossary, and index."—Provided by publisher.
Identifiers: LCCN 2021062168 (print) |
LCCN 2021062169 (ebook) |
ISBN 9781645493112 (hardcover) |
ISBN 9781681528359 (paperback) |
ISBN 9781645493990 (ebook)
Subjects: LCSH: Turtles as pets–Juvenile literature.
Classification: LCC SF459.T8 T45 2023
(print) | LCC SF459.T8 (ebook) |
DDC 639.3/92–dc23/eng/20220119
LC record available at https://lccn.loc.gov/2021062168
LC ebook record available at https://lccn.loc.gov/2021062169

Photo Credits: Dreamstime/Maryna Kolechyna 17;
iStock/baxterdogy247 18–19, Belikart 14, iStock/
Captainflash 17, chengyuzheng 17, cpaulfell 11, GlobalP
12–13, 15, imv 17, jjneff 10, joecicak cover, lighty25 1,
15, mactrunk 15; Shutterstock/Aliaksandr Bukatsich 2,
8–9, Charlotte Bleijenberg 6–7, Eugenie Robitaille 2, 5,
Mendelex 17, reptiles4all 15, Shvoeva Elena 3, 21

What makes a turtle a good pet?

Turtles are not cuddly. They won't play fetch or curl up in your lap. But they can be beautiful pets. They live a long time. They don't have to be walked. And it's fun to watch them swim around.

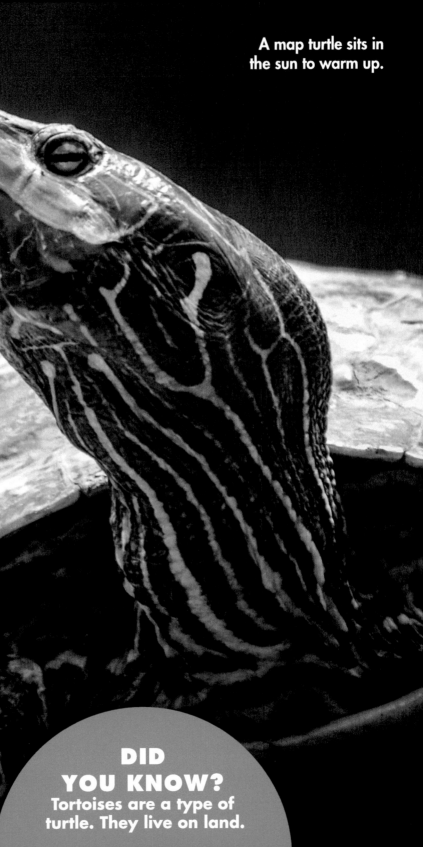

A map turtle sits in the sun to warm up.

DID YOU KNOW?
Tortoises are a type of turtle. They live on land.

Where do you keep a pet turtle?

Indoors, you need a large aquarium. A filter keeps the water clean. The turtle also needs a land area. It will **bask** there under a heat lamp. The tank should be a toasty 80 °F (26.7 °C). An outdoor pond is another option, but only in warm weather.

A turtle tank can look like a pond with rocks and plants.

Can I pick up my turtle?

Move slowly if you need to pick up your turtle. It may bite.

Yes. But this can stress out turtles, so don't do it all the time. You should also be careful. Turtles often carry **salmonella**. It makes humans sick. Wash your hands after touching a turtle.

A box turtle has yellow or orange markings on its shell.

How do I tell if my turtle is a boy or a girl?

It can be hard to know. Ask a veterinarian to be sure. Tail length is often the easiest way to tell. Females have a shorter, skinnier tail. A male's tail is longer and thicker. Females have bigger shells. They are flat on the bottom. A male's shell is curved on the bottom. Males also have longer front claws.

Turtles pile on each other to get more sun.

DID YOU KNOW?

A female turtle can lay eggs. Unless she has mated, the eggs won't hatch.

Can a turtle take its shell off?

No. The shell is made of keratin, like your fingernails. The top part is the carapace. It is attached to the spine and ribs. It is covered by hard **scutes**. As the turtle grows, so does its shell. New scutes grow. The old ones may shed off. A turtle keeps the same shell its whole life.

A turtle's shell protects its soft body.

DID YOU KNOW?
A turtle can feel pressure and pain through its shell.

How big will my turtle get?

Turtles grow slowly. It can take 8 years for them to reach full size. Most turtles are about 6 inches (15 cm) long. A red-eared slider can grow to 1 foot (0.3 m). Turtles are a long-term pet. They live about 30 years. A box turtle can live 50 years!

EASTERN BOX
TURTLE
50+ YEARS

PAINTED
TURTLE
25–30 years

RED-EARED
SLIDER
20–30 YEARS

YELLOW-BELLIED
SLIDER
30–40 YEARS

TEXAS
MAP TURTLE
30–40 YEARS

What do turtles do?

Turtles swim and eat. They bask for hours. Some turtles are diggers. They use their claws to dig in sand and dirt. Turtles are very active. Some are awake at night. Others are awake during the day.

Turtles love to swim.

WHAT DO TURTLES EAT?

Spinach

Insects

Pellets

Small fish

Why does my turtle hiss?

It is scared. See how its head is pulled back into its shell? This action pushes the air in its lungs out. A hissing sound is made. A turtle may "hiss" when you try to pet them. You may have startled it. Or it doesn't like to be touched.

A turtle could not survive without its shell.

DID YOU KNOW?
You can take your pet turtle outside to explore!

Can turtles breathe under water?

No. Turtles need to breathe air. Most turtles can hold their breath for 30 minutes. Painted turtles can hold their breath for hours. They even sleep under water. They lower their heart rate and **digestion**. This uses less energy, so they need less oxygen.

Webbed feet help
turtles swim well.

DID
YOU KNOW?
Wild turtles hibernate
under water. They take
oxygen from the water
through their butt.

ASK MORE QUESTIONS

How do I make an outdoor pond for my turtle?

What do I need to take care of a turtle?

**Try a BIG QUESTION:
Why do people take turtles from the wild?**

SEARCH FOR ANSWERS

Search the library catalog or the Internet.
A librarian, teacher, or parent can help you.

Using Keywords
Find the looking glass.

$\mathcal{Q}$

Keywords are the most important words in your question.

?

If you want to know about:

- how to build an outdoor turtle pond, type: TURTLE POND HOW TO

- what you need for a pet turtle, type: PET TURTLE SUPPLY LIST

FIND GOOD SOURCES

Here are some good, safe sources you can use in your research.
Your librarian can help you find more.

Books

Is a Turtle a Good Pet for Me?
by Therese M. Shea, 2020.

Is It a Turtle or a Tortoise?
by Gail Terp, 2020.

Internet Sites

Turtle Care 101
*www.petmd.com/reptile/care/
evr_rp_how-to-take-care-of-pet-turtles*
PetMD has articles written by veterinarians. It is a great resource for pet information.

What You Need for a Turtle Pond
www.thesprucepets.com/aquatic-turtles-and-outdoor-ponds-1238361
The Spruce Pets publishes articles about pets. It is reviewed by veterinarians.

Every effort has been made to ensure that these websites are appropriate for children. However, because of the nature of the Internet, it is impossible to guarantee that these sites will remain active indefinitely or that their contents will not be altered.

SHARE AND TAKE ACTION

Look for wild turtles in a pond.
Remember to not take any animals from their natural habitat.

Visit turtles at an aquarium.
How many species do they have? How are they all different?

Help a turtle rescue organization.
Some take in pet turtles who need a new home, while others help wild turtles.

GLOSSARY

bask To lie or relax in a warm place.

digestion The process of food being used by the body for energy.

hibernate When an animal spends the winter in a deep sleep.

mate When a male and female animal join together to make young.

salmonella A bacteria that causes food poisoning in humans.

scute A thick plate on a turtle's shell that is made of keratin.

INDEX

About the Author

Alissa Thielges is a writer and editor in southern Minnesota who hopes to inspire kids to stay curious about their interests. She doesn't own any pets but would love to have a turtle and dog someday.